Know Your States!

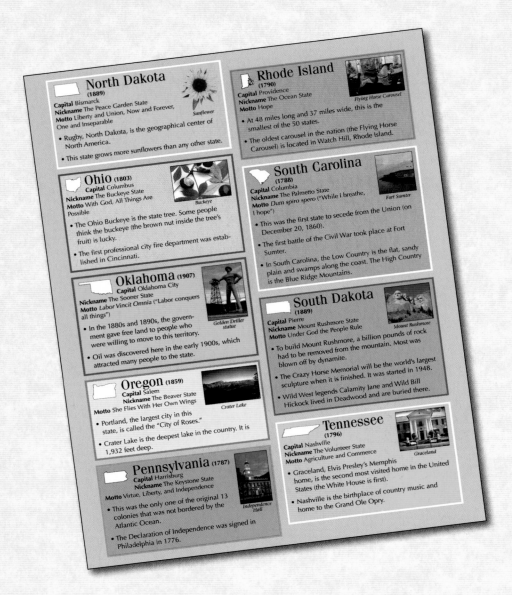

North Dakota (1889)

Capital Bismarck
Nickname The Peace Garden State
Motto Liberty and Union, Now and Forever, One and Inseparable

Sunflower

- Rugby, North Dakota, is the geographical center of North America.
- This state grows more sunflowers than any other state.

Ohio (1803)

Capital Columbus
Nickname The Buckeye State
Motto With God, All Things Are Possible

Buckeye

- The Ohio Buckeye is the state tree. Some people think the buckeye (the brown nut inside the tree's fruit) is lucky.
- The first professional city fire department was established in Cincinnati.

Oklahoma (1907)

Capital Oklahoma City
Nickname The Sooner State
Motto *Labor Vincit Omnia* ("Labor conquers all things")

Golden Driller statue

- In the 1880s and 1890s, the government gave free land to people who were willing to move to this territory.
- Oil was discovered here in the early 1900s, which attracted many people to the state.

Oregon (1859)

Capital Salem
Nickname The Beaver State
Motto She Flies With Her Own Wings

Crater Lake

- Portland, the largest city in this state, is called the "City of Roses."
- Crater Lake is the deepest lake in the country. It is 1,932 feet deep.

Pennsylvania (1787)

Capital Harrisburg
Nickname The Keystone State
Motto Virtue, Liberty, and Independence

Independence Hall

- This was the only one of the original 13 colonies that was not bordered by the Atlantic Ocean.
- The Declaration of Independence was signed in Philadelphia in 1776.

Rhode Island (1790)

Capital Providence
Nickname The Ocean State
Motto Hope

Flying Horse Carousel

- At 48 miles long and 37 miles wide, this is the smallest of the 50 states.
- The oldest carousel in the nation (the Flying Horse Carousel) is located in Watch Hill, Rhode Island.

South Carolina (1788)

Capital Columbia
Nickname The Palmetto State
Motto *Dum spiro spero* ("While I breathe, I hope")

Fort Sumter

- This was the first state to secede from the Union (on December 20, 1860).
- The first battle of the Civil War took place at Fort Sumter.
- In South Carolina, the Low Country is the flat, sandy plain and swamps along the coast. The High Country is the Blue Ridge Mountains.

South Dakota (1889)

Capital Pierre
Nickname Mount Rushmore State
Motto Under God the People Rule

Mount Rushmore

- To build Mount Rushmore, a billion pounds of rock had to be removed from the mountain. Most was blown off by dynamite.
- The Crazy Horse Memorial will be the world's largest sculpture when it is finished. It was started in 1948.
- Wild West legends Calamity Jane and Wild Bill Hickock lived in Deadwood and are buried there.

Tennessee (1796)

Capital Nashville
Nickname The Volunteer State
Motto Agriculture and Commerce

Graceland

- Graceland, Elvis Presley's Memphis home, is the second most visited home in the United States (the White House is first).
- Nashville is the birthplace of country music and home to the Grand Ole Opry.

★ The 7-panel foldout wall chart is perforated to detach from the book.

★ Children will learn many fascinating facts about the 50 states and Washington, D.C.

★ A colorful map shows state capitals and regional breakdowns.

Map of the United States

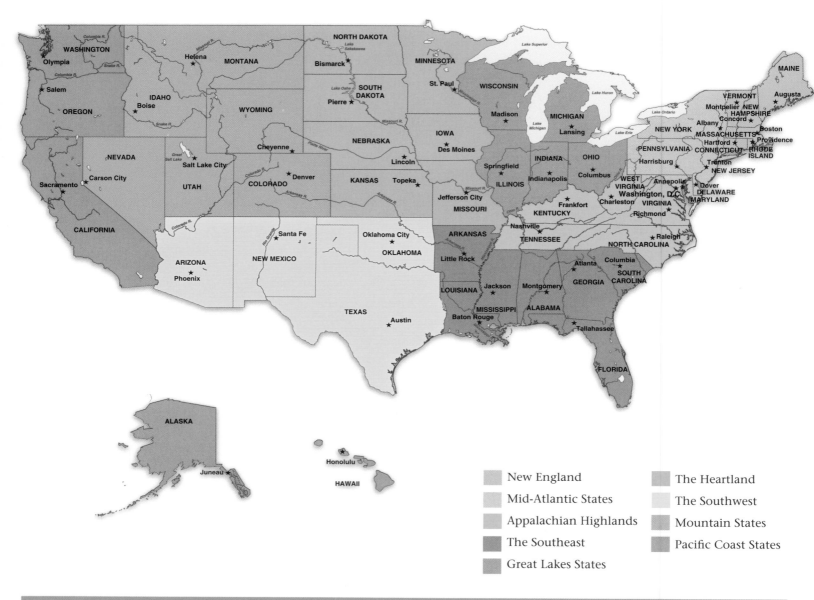

New England

Mid-Atlantic States

Appalachian Highlands

The Southeast

Great Lakes States

The Heartland

The Southwest

Mountain States

Pacific Coast States

Washington, D.C. (1790)

Capital Washington, D.C., is the capital of the United States of America

Nickname Capital City

Motto *Justitia Omnibus* ("Justice for All")

- The first name suggested for the district was "Washingtonople."

- The name Washington, D.C., honors both the first president of the United States and explorer Christopher Columbus. That's where *District of Columbia* comes from.

- The district's site was selected by President George Washington, partly because it was so close to his home, Mount Vernon.

The Capitol

Texas (1845)

Capital Austin
Nickname The Lone Star State
Motto Friendship

The Alamo

- The Alamo in San Antonio is thought of as the cradle of Texas liberty. It is the state's most popular historic site.
- More than 1.5 million Mexican free-tailed bats live under a bridge in Austin.
- Tortilla chips and salsa is the official state snack of Texas.

Utah (1896)

Capital Salt Lake City
Nickname The Beehive State
Motto Industry

Arches National Park

- More than 2,000 sandstone arches are located at Arches National Park in Utah.
- Utah's Great Salt Lake is even saltier than the oceans.
- Brigham Young led a group of Mormons to Salt Lake City in 1847. Today, Utah is known for its large Mormon population and historic sites such as Temple Square.

Vermont (1791)

Capital Montpelier
Nickname The Green Mountain State
Motto Freedom and Unity

Covered bridge

- Vermont produces the most maple syrup in the United States.
- There are more than 100 covered bridges in this state.

Virginia (1788)

Capital Richmond
Nickname Old Dominion
Motto *Sic Semper Tyrannis* ("Thus Always to Tyrants")

Monticello

- In 1607, the first permanent English settlement in America was established at Jamestown.
- Virginia is called the Mother of States: All or part of eight other states were formed from land that was once part of Virginia.
- George Washington's home, Mount Vernon, and Thomas Jefferson's home, Monticello, are in Virginia.

Washington (1889)

Capital Olympia
Nickname The Evergreen State
Motto *Al-ki* ("Bye and bye")

Apple tree

- Washington is the only state named after a U.S. President (George Washington, of course).
- This state produces more apples than any other state in the country.

West Virginia (1863)

Capital Charleston
Nickname The Mountain State
Motto *Montani Semper Liberi* ("Mountaineers Are Always Free")

Appalachian Mountains

- West Virginia was once part of Virginia but broke away over the issue of slavery to form its own state.
- Most people in this state live in rural areas, and nearly 75 percent of the state is covered by forests.
- The whole state lies within the Appalachian Mountain range.

Wisconsin (1848)

Capital Madison
Nickname The Badger State
Motto Forward

Dairy cow

- Wisconsin is the dairy capital of the United States. It produces more cheese and more milk than any other state.
- Lead miners in the mid-1800s lived in caves they dug in the sides of hills—just as badgers do. That's how the state got its nickname, the Badger State.

Wyoming (1890)

Capital Cheyenne
Nickname The Equality State
Motto Equal Rights

Yellowstone National Park

- In 1869, this state passed the first law that gave women the right to vote and hold public office.
- Wyoming has fewer people than any other state.
- In 1872, Yellowstone became the first official National Park in the United States.

Louis Weber, CEO
Publications International, Ltd.
7373 North Cicero Avenue
Lincolnwood, Illinois 60712

Permission is never granted for commercial purposes.

ISBN-13: 978-1-4127-1333-7
ISBN-10: 1-4127-1333-1

Manufactured in China.

8 7 6 5 4 3 2 1

Montana (1889)

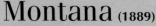

Capital Helena
Nickname The Treasure State
Motto *Oro y Plata* ("Gold and Silver")

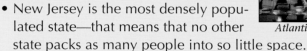
Big Sky Country

- Montana is big, but it has a small population. There are only about six people per square mile in some counties.

- Montana is sometimes called the Big Sky Country.

- Glacier National Park is the most visited place in the state.

Nebraska (1867)

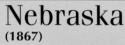

Capital Lincoln
Nickname The Cornhusker State
Motto Equality before the law

Fort Robinson

- Today, farmland and ranches cover about 95 percent of the state.

- The 911 emergency system, now used nationwide, was developed and first used in Lincoln, Nebraska.

- Nebraska has five army forts open to the public: Atkinson, Kearny, Hartsuff, Sidney, and Robinson.

Nevada (1864)

Capital Carson City
Nickname The Silver State
Motto All for our Country

Las Vegas

- The average annual rainfall in Nevada is only seven inches. That's the least amount of rainfall of any state.

- Gambling was legalized in this state in March 1931.

- Nevada has more mountain ranges than any other state.

New Hampshire (1788)

Capital Concord
Nickname The Granite State
Motto Live Free or Die

The Capitol

- This state was named after the town of Hampshire, England.

- The first free public library in the United States was established in Peterborough in 1833.

- Mystery Hill in Salem is a 4,000-year-old site that is known as America's version of Stonehenge.

New Jersey (1787)

Capital Trenton
Nickname The Garden State
Motto Liberty and Prosperity

Atlantic City

- New Jersey is the most densely populated state—that means that no other state packs as many people into so little space.

- The longest boardwalk in the world is in Atlantic City on the Jersey shore.

- Thomas Edison invented the lightbulb, the phonograph, and the motion picture projector in his laboratory in Menlo Park.

New Mexico (1912)

Capital Santa Fe
Nickname The Land of Enchantment
Motto *Crescit Eundo* ("It Grows As It Goes")

Hot air balloons

- The northwest corner of New Mexico meets the corners of three other states: Arizona, Utah, and Colorado.

- The world's largest international hot air balloon festival is held each October in Albuquerque.

New York (1788)

Capital Albany
Nickname The Empire State
Motto *Excelsior!* ("Ever Upward!")

The Empire State Building

- There are 722 miles of subway track in New York City.

- The colony first settled here by the Dutch was called New Netherland. When the English took it over, they renamed it New York in honor of the Duke of York.

- The National Baseball Hall of Fame is located in Cooperstown, in upstate New York.

North Carolina (1789)

Capital Raleigh
Nickname The Tar Heel State
Motto *Esse Quam Videri* ("To be, rather than to seem")

Kitty Hawk

- North Carolina's Outer Banks are called the Graveyard of the Atlantic because more than 2,000 ships have wrecked there.

- The Wright brothers made the first successful airplane flight over Kitty Hawk on December 17, 1903.

North Dakota
(1889)

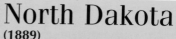

Capital Bismarck
Nickname The Peace Garden State
Motto Liberty and Union, Now and Forever, One and Inseparable

Sunflower

- Rugby, North Dakota, is the geographical center of North America.

- This state grows more sunflowers than any other state.

Ohio (1803)

Capital Columbus
Nickname The Buckeye State
Motto With God, All Things Are Possible

Buckeye leaves and nuts

- The Ohio Buckeye is the state tree. Some people think the buckeye (the brown nut inside the tree's fruit) is lucky.

- The first professional city fire department was established in Cincinnati.

Oklahoma (1907)

Capital Oklahoma City
Nickname The Sooner State
Motto *Labor Vincit Omnia* ("Labor conquers all things")

Golden Driller statue

- In the 1880s and 1890s, the government gave free land to people who were willing to move to this territory.

- Oil was discovered here in the early 1900s, which attracted many people to the state.

Oregon (1859)

Capital Salem
Nickname The Beaver State
Motto She Flies With Her Own Wings

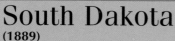
Crater Lake

- Portland, the largest city in this state, is called the City of Roses.

- Crater Lake is the deepest lake in the country. It is 1,932 feet deep.

Pennsylvania (1787)

Capital Harrisburg
Nickname The Keystone State
Motto Virtue, Liberty, and Independence

Independence Hall

- This was the only one of the original 13 colonies that was not bordered by the Atlantic Ocean.

- The Declaration of Independence was signed in Philadelphia in 1776.

Rhode Island
(1790)

Capital Providence
Nickname The Ocean State
Motto Hope

Flying Horse Carousel

- At 48 miles long and 37 miles wide, this is the smallest of the 50 states.

- The oldest carousel in the nation (the Flying Horse Carousel) is located in Watch Hill, Rhode Island.

South Carolina
(1788)

Capital Columbia
Nickname The Palmetto State
Motto *Dum spiro spero* ("While I breathe, I hope")

Fort Sumter

- This was the first state to secede from the Union (on December 20, 1860).

- The first battle of the Civil War took place at Fort Sumter.

- In South Carolina, the Low Country is the flat, sandy plain and swamps along the coast. The High Country is the Blue Ridge Mountains.

South Dakota
(1889)

Capital Pierre
Nickname Mount Rushmore State
Motto Under God the People Rule

Mount Rushmore

- To build Mount Rushmore, a billion pounds of rock had to be removed from the mountain. Most was blown off by dynamite.

- The Crazy Horse Memorial will be the world's largest sculpture when it is finished. It was started in 1948.

- Wild West legends Calamity Jane and Wild Bill Hickok lived in Deadwood and are buried there.

Tennessee
(1796)

Capital Nashville
Nickname The Volunteer State
Motto Agriculture and Commerce

Graceland

- Graceland, Elvis Presley's Memphis home, is the second most visited home in the United States (the White House is first).

- Nashville is the birthplace of country music and home to the Grand Ole Opry.

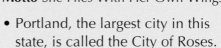

Georgia (1788)
Capital Atlanta
Nickname The Peach State
Motto Wisdom, Justice, and Moderation

"P" is for peanuts

- Civil rights leader Martin Luther King, Jr., was born in Atlanta.
- Georgia is the country's top producer of the three Ps: peanuts, pecans, and peaches.
- Coca-Cola was invented in Atlanta in 1886.

Indiana (1816)
Capital Indianapolis
Nickname The Hoosier State
Motto The Crossroads of America

Indy 500

- *Indiana* means "land of the Indians," but fewer than 8,000 Native Americans live in the state today.
- Indianapolis Motor Speedway is home to "The Greatest Spectacle in Racing"—the Indianapolis 500

Hawaii (1959)
Capital Honolulu
Nickname The Aloha State
Motto *Ua mau ke ea o ka aina i ka pono* ("The life of the land is perpetuated in righteousness")

Kilauea

- Hawaii is made up of eight major islands. Early Hawaiians thought that one of them, Kahoolawe, was the center of the universe.
- There are two active volcanoes in Hawaii: Kilauea and Mauna Loa.

Iowa (1846)
Capital Des Moines
Nickname The Hawkeye State
Motto Our liberties we prize, and our rights we will maintain

Corn

- The land that is now Iowa was part of the Louisiana Purchase in 1803.
- Iowa is called the Land Where the Tall Corn Grows.
- Fort Atkinson was the only fort ever built by the U.S. government to protect one Indian nation from another.

Idaho (1890)
Capital Boise
Nickname The Gem State
Motto *Esto Perpetua* ("Let it be Perpetual")

Hells Canyon

- More potatoes are grown in this state than in any other.
- There are more than 2,000 lakes and more than 16,000 miles of rivers in Idaho.
- Hells Canyon is the deepest gorge in America.

Kansas (1861)
Capital Topeka
Nickname The Sunflower State
Motto *Ad Astra Per Aspera* ("To the Stars Through Difficulties")

Geographic Center Lebanon, Kansas

- The exact middle of the lower 48 states is just outside Lebanon, Kansas.
- The windiest city in the United States is Dodge City, Kansas.
- Kansas leads the nation in wheat production. The state is called the Breadbasket of America.

Illinois (1818)
Capital Springfield
Nickname The Prairie State
Motto State Sovereignty, National Union

Abraham Lincoln

- More than half of the people in Illinois live in or near Chicago.
- The state's official slogan is "Land of Lincoln" because Abraham Lincoln lived and worked here most of his life.
- The ice-cream sundae was invented in Evanston,

Kentucky (1792)
Capital Frankfort
Nickname The Bluegrass State
Motto *Deo gratiam habeamus* ("Let us be grateful to God")

Mammoth Cave

- $6 trillion worth of gold is held in the underground vaults of Fort Knox.
- Mammoth Cave is the longest cave system in the world, with more than 340 miles of passageways and five levels.
- Middlesboro, Kentucky, is the only city in the United States built within a meteor crater.

Louisiana (1812)

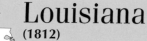

Capital Baton Rouge
Nickname The Pelican State
Motto Union, Justice, Confidence

Mardi Gras, New Orleans

- Louisiana was named in 1682 to honor King Louis XIV of France.

- In the Louisiana Purchase of 1803, the United States purchased Louisiana and parts of 13 other states from France for $15 million, doubling the size of the country.

Michigan (1837)

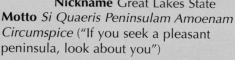

Capital Lansing
Nickname Great Lakes State
Motto *Si Quaeris Peninsulam Amoenam Circumspice* ("If you seek a pleasant peninsula, look about you")

Henry Ford Museum

- More cars and trucks are manufactured in Michigan than in any other state.

- Michigan is called the Wolverine State, but today there are no wolverines in Michigan.

- Michigan has two parts that are separated by water: the Upper Peninsula and the Lower Peninsula.

Maine (1820)

Capital Augusta
Nickname The Pine Tree State
Motto *Dirigo* ("I lead")

Portland Head Light

- The Portland Head Light at Cape Elizabeth, Maine, is one of the oldest lighthouses in America. It was completed in 1791.

- About 40 million pounds of lobsters are caught off the coast of Maine every year.

Minnesota (1858)

Capital St. Paul
Nickname The North Star State
Motto *L'etoile du Nord* ("Star of the North")

Mall of America

- This state, sometimes called the Land of 10,000 Lakes, actually has more than 15,000 lakes.

- International Falls is known as the coldest place in the continental United States.

- The Mall of America in Bloomington, Minnesota, is the size of 78 football fields.

Maryland (1788)

Capital Annapolis
Nickname The Old Line State
Motto *Fatti Maschii, Parole Femine* ("Manly Deeds, Womanly Words")

Annapolis

- During the War of 1812, in Baltimore, Francis Scott Key wrote "The Star Spangled Banner," which became the national anthem.

- The Chesapeake Bay runs through the state, almost dividing it in half.

- Annapolis was once the capital of the United States.

Mississippi (1817)

Capital Jackson
Nickname The Magnolia State
Motto *Virtute et Armis* ("By Valor and Arms")

Civil rights march

- Many civil rights marches were held in Mississippi in the 1960s.

- Greenwood, Mississippi, is called the Cotton Capital of the World.

- Elvis Presley was born in Tupelo, Mississippi.

Massachusetts (1788)

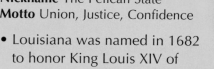

Capital Boston
Nickname The Bay State
Motto *Ense Petit Placidam Sub Libertate Quietem* ("By the Sword We Seek Peace, But Peace Only Under Liberty")

Basketball

- The first Thanksgiving was celebrated in Plymouth in 1621.

- James Naismith invented basketball in Springfield, Massachusetts, in 1891.

- The first subway system in the United States was started in Boston in 1897.

Missouri (1821)

Capital Jefferson City
Nickname The Show-Me State
Motto *Salus Populi Suprema Lex Esto* ("Let the welfare of the people be the supreme law")

The Gateway Arch

- Lewis and Clark started their exploration of the United States in Missouri.

- The Gateway Arch in St. Louis is 630 feet tall and is the tallest monument in the United States.

- Hannibal, Missouri, was home to writer Mark Twain and was the setting for *The Adventures of Tom Sawyer*.

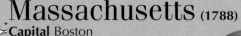
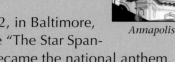

Alabama (1819)

Capital Montgomery
Nickname The Heart of Dixie
Motto *Audemus jura nostra defendere* ("We Dare Maintain Our Rights")

Rosa Parks

- Montgomery, Alabama, was the birthplace and capital of the Confederate States of America.

- In December 1955, African-American Rosa Parks was arrested in Montgomery for refusing to give up her seat on a bus to a white man, resulting in the first formal protest of the civil rights movement.

Alaska (1959)

Capital Juneau
Nickname The Last Frontier
Motto North to the Future

Iditarod

- Alaska has approximately 100,000 glaciers; 60 are within 50 miles of Anchorage.

- The Iditarod is a famous dogsled race that covers more than 1,000 miles and takes about 10 days to complete.

Arizona (1912)

Capital Phoenix
Nickname The Grand Canyon State
Motto *Ditat Deus* ("God Enriches")

The Grand Canyon

- Arizona has 20 Native American reservations. They cover about one-fourth of the state.

- The *youngest* rock layer in the Grand Canyon in Arizona is 250 million years old; the oldest is almost 2 billion years old!

- The amount of copper on the roof of Arizona's capitol building is equivalent to 4,800,000 pennies.

Arkansas (1836)

Capital Little Rock
Nickname The Natural State
Motto *Regnat Populus* ("The People Rule")

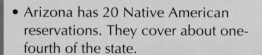

Diamond

- Arkansas had both a Union and a Confederate government from 1863 until the Civil War ended.

- You can actually dig for diamonds in Crater of Diamonds State Park—and take home whatever you find!

- There are 47 springs in Hot Springs National Park that have a water temperature of 143°F.

California (1850)

Capital Sacramento
Nickname The Golden State
Motto *Eureka!* ("I have found it!")

General Sherman tree

- In 1849, the Gold Rush caused California's population to increase from 15,000 to more than 100,000.

- The General Sherman tree in Sequoia National Park is the largest tree in the world. It's almost 275 feet tall!

Colorado (1876)

Capital Denver
Nickname Centennial State
Motto *Nil Sine Numine* ("Nothing without Providence")

Coins from the U.S. Mint

- In 2004, the U.S. Mint in Denver produced a total of 6,546,940,000 coins.

- Denver is called the Mile High City because it is exactly one mile above sea level.

Connecticut (1788)

Capital Hartford
Nickname The Constitution State
Motto *Qui Transtulit Sustinet* ("He who transplanted still sustains")

Patriot Nathan Hale

- Connecticut is the third-smallest state. It could fit inside Alaska almost 300 times.

- The first public library and newspaper in the United States were started in Connecticut.

Delaware (1787)

Capital Dover
Nickname The First State
Motto Liberty and Independence

U.S. Constitution

- Delaware is the only state that has no national parks.

- Delaware is called The First State because it was the first state to approve the U.S. Constitution.

Florida (1845)

Capital Tallahassee
Nickname The Sunshine State
Motto In God We Trust

Florida oranges

- Throughout its history, Florida has been a part of five different countries: Spain, France, Great Britain, the United States, and the Confederate States of America.

- Florida grows more oranges than any other state—about 252 million boxes of oranges per year!

States

The People, Landmarks, and Highlights of the 50 States

Contents

Copyright © 2007 Publications International, Ltd. All rights reserved. This book may not be reproduced or quoted in whole or in part by any means whatsoever without written permission from:

Louis Weber, CEO
Publications International, Ltd.
7373 North Cicero Avenue
Lincolnwood, Illinois 60712

Permission is never granted for commercial purposes.

ISBN-13: 978-1-4127-1334-4
ISBN-10: 1-4127-1334-X

Manufactured in China.

8 7 6 5 4 3 2 1

Suzanne Lieurance is a freelance writer and children's author. She has published more than 12 books for children and is currently at work on a historical middle grade novel. She is a master teacher at the online University of Masters, where she teaches a telecourse called Freelance Writers: How to Jumpstart Your Career. Visit her Web site at www.suzannelieurance.com for more information about her books.

Facts verified by **Regina Montgomery**.

Alabama

For 250 years the Spanish, the French, and the British fought over the area that is now Alabama. After the American Revolution, which ended in 1776, most of Alabama came under the control of the United States, even though the Spanish kept the coastal Mobile area until 1813. Alabama became a territory in 1817 and a state in 1819.

Alabama is named for the Alibamu people. Birmingham is the state's largest city, and Montgomery is the capital. In 1955, Dr. Martin Luther King, Jr., asked African-Americans to stop riding the buses in Montgomery. This was the beginning of the civil rights movement in the United States.

Alabama helped launch the space age. The George C. Marshall Space Center was built in Huntsville in 1960, and rockets developed there took astronauts into space. Many famous Americans were born in Alabama, including Helen Keller, boxer Joe Louis, and baseball great Hank Aaron.

Sitting Down to Take a Stand

In December 1955, African-American Rosa Parks stood up for her rights when she refused to give up her seat on a Montgomery bus to a white man. Her arrest led to a formal boycott of buses in Montgomery.

In the early 1900s, most of Alabama's cotton crop was destroyed by insects called boll weevils. Farmers were forced to grow other crops, which, oddly enough, made them more money than cotton did. The people of Alabama built a statue honoring the boll weevil and its contribution to the state's economy.

Alaska

Alaska is the largest state in the country. In fact, it is as big as one-fifth of the rest of the United States!

Today Alaska has much to be proud of. But Americans weren't so proud of this area when Secretary of State William Seward bought Alaska from Russia in 1867. Seward paid $7,200,000 for all of Alaska. That's only about two cents an acre. But even at that low price people laughed at Seward and nicknamed Alaska "Seward's Icebox" and "Seward's Folly." However, they soon realized the vast natural resources in Alaska, such as natural gas, oil, fish, furs, whales, and copper. Thousands of people rushed to the territory in 1898 when gold was discovered. People no longer laugh about Seward's purchase!

Alaska became the 49th state in 1959. It contains the largest national park, the largest national forest, and the largest state park in the United States. Mount McKinley, the highest peak in North America, is also in Alaska.

Alaska's flag was designed in 1926 by a 13-year-old Aleut boy named Bennie Benson.

There are approximately 100,000 glaciers in Alaska.

Arizona

Arizona was part of Mexico when the Spanish first came there searching for gold in 1539. Many Native American nations, such as the Hopi, Navajo, and Apache, lived there. The Spaniards didn't find the gold they were after, but they did find land with distinctive deserts and amazing structures of red sandstone. The Spanish controlled this land until 1848, when the war between the United States and Mexico ended and the United States acquired most of Arizona.

After the Civil War, Arizona became part of what was known as the Wild West. Gold, silver, and copper were mined there, and mining towns that cropped up were often wild, lawless communities. The people who lived in them did not want Arizona to become a state. It finally did become a state in 1912. Since that time, Arizona has changed a lot. Dams were built to give residents a steady supply of water, and when air-conditioning was invented, Arizona became a comfortable place for people to live all year long.

The saguaro is the largest cactus in the United States.

President Theodore Roosevelt called the Grand Canyon "the one great sight which every American should see." This natural wonder in northern Arizona is a mile deep and more than 200 miles long.

Arkansas

Arkansas has 47 springs that have a natural water temperature of 143 degrees. Visitors from around the world flock to these springs to bathe in their thermal waters. According to legend, warring Native American nations used to lay down their arms to bathe in the healing waters of what is now Hot Springs, Arkansas.

The early French explorers made up the word *Arkansas* to describe the Quapaw people and the river they lived on. It means "downriver people." The state earned one of its nicknames, "land of opportunities," in the 1800s, when jobs in the railroad, mining, paper, and farming industries were plentiful. In 1836, Arkansas became the 25th state.

Today there are still many opportunities for work—and play—in Arkansas. Dairy products, lumber, paper, petroleum, rice, and soybeans are all produced or grown in Arkansas. Fishing, hiking, and boating are just some of the many pastimes enjoyed by residents as well as tourists.

Finders Keepers

In Murfreesboro, Arkansas, you can look for diamonds in Crater of Diamonds State Park. The policy in the park's diamond searching area is "finders keepers." Any diamonds, semiprecious stones, rocks, or minerals you uncover there are yours to keep.

California

Four of the largest cities in the United States (Los Angeles, San Diego, San Jose, and San Francisco) are located in California. Sacramento, the capital, is also a large city.

The Hollywood sign in the mountains above Los Angeles is a symbol of the movie industry.

From sandy beaches and rocky oceanside cliffs to barren deserts, rich forests, and snowy mountain peaks, California has it all. California is the third largest state, but it has the largest population of any state. The highest waterfall in all of North America is in California's Yosemite National Park, and the world's tallest living tree is in Redwood National Park. The highest temperature ever recorded in the United States was 134° Fahrenheit, recorded in July 1913 in California's Death Valley.

Native Americans have lived in the area that is now California for thousands of years. In 1579, English and Spanish explorers began visiting the coast. Many of these Europeans came searching for wealth. Some of them were looking for a mythical sea route through the Americas to Asia. Others came looking for gold.

In 1821, California became part of Mexico. In 1846, the United States went to war with Mexico. When the United States won the war, it bought California. That year gold was found in California and people poured into the area.

In 1850, California became the 31st state. Today it is called the Golden State because of its bright, sunny days and memories of the gold rush that caused so many people to move there long ago.

The Crookedest Street in the World

Lombard Street in San Francisco is known as "the crookedest street in the world." A one-block section of this street has eight sharp turns, called "switchbacks," that were created to reduce the hill's natural 27-degree slope. It was too steep for most vehicles to climb and too dangerous for pedestrians.

California Fun

It's easy to have fun in California! The state has more amusement parks and theme parks than any other state. Disneyland (shown) and Knott's Berry Farm are two of California's most famous parks.

3

Colorado

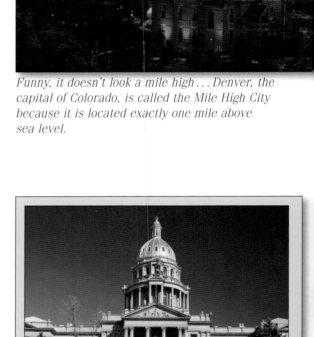

The earliest inhabitants of Colorado were Native Americans. Many of them lived in cliff dwellings (built more than 700 years ago), which visitors can still see today at Mesa Verde National Park. The name *Colorado* comes from Spanish. It means "colored red," and refers to the red stone canyons Spanish explorers discovered there in the 1600s.

Back in the mid-1800s, gold was found near Pikes Peak, a famous mountain in Colorado. People rushed to the area, but most of them did not find gold. Instead, they became farmers and settled along the eastern edge of the Rocky Mountains. By 1870, the motto was "Go west, young man!" After Colorado became a state in 1876, prospectors again raced to the area. This time, they were searching for silver. In 1894, the biggest piece of silver ever found in North America was mined in Aspen. It weighed 1,840 pounds!

Today, gold, silver, and coal are still mined in Colorado. But the state is also home to cattle ranches and many other industries.

People come from all over to ski and snowboard down the many slopes, and the hiking trails are among the most beautiful in the country.

Funny, it doesn't look a mile high... Denver, the capital of Colorado, is called the Mile High City because it is located exactly one mile above sea level.

Every year since 1916, daring drivers and motorcycle riders have raced 12.4 miles on Pikes Peak Highway to the 14,100-foot summit of Pikes Peak in a race to the clouds. The racers face hairpin curves around 2,000-foot cliffs with no guardrails.

The U.S. Air Force Academy near Colorado Springs trains people to be officers in the United States Air Force.

Seeing Red

Amazingly, it took six years (1894–1900) to cut, polish, and install the red marble, called "Beulah red," in the Colorado State Capitol. Even more amazing is the fact that all of the "Beulah red" marble in the world went into this one magnificent building, making it simply irreplaceable.

Connecticut

Connecticut is the third smallest state in the country. In fact, it's so small, it could fit inside Alaska almost 300 times!

It may be small, but Connecticut has many historical firsts to be proud of. In 1639, Connecticut adopted the first written constitution, which is why it is called the Constitution State. It became the fifth state in 1788. The first hamburger (1895), the first lollipop (1908), and the first color TV (1948) all came from Connecticut. Connecticut also had the first public library and produced the first newspaper.

By the 1800s, cities quickly sprang up around the state's many factories. Yet today, Connecticut is still known for its lovely small towns and villages.

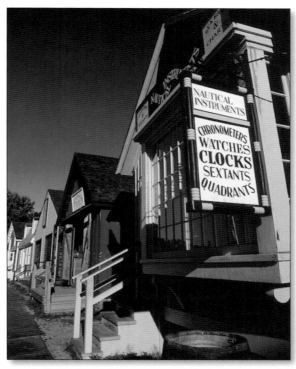

Connecticut still offers old-fashioned charm in many of its small towns.

Delaware

Delaware's soldiers carried fighting roosters into battle. The roosters' mother was a blue hen, so the soldiers called themselves "Blue Hen's Chickens." Today, the blue hen chicken is Delaware's state bird.

The first Europeans who settled in Delaware came from Sweden and Finland. They made their homes in the area that is now Wilmington. They built log cabins, which people in this country had never seen before.

After the Revolutionary War, when the country's leaders wrote the U.S. Constitution, Delaware was the first state to adopt it. For that reason, Delaware's nickname is the First State.

Today, Wilmington is Delaware's largest city and is known as the "Chemical Capital of the World" because of all the chemical factories there. But farming is also an important industry in Delaware. Soybeans and chickens are two of the most popular agricultural products raised in this state.

The Winterthur Garden—within an American country estate—has 60 acres of beautiful flowers.

Florida

Florida grows more oranges than any other state—about 252 million boxes of oranges per year!

A Spaniard named Juan Ponce de Leon came to Florida in 1513 searching for a fountain of youth. He never found it. But he did find plenty of natural beauty, including many rivers and lakes, and a vast wetland that is now famous and is called the Everglades. Here, Ponce de Leon saw many amazing animals, including panthers, alligators, crocodiles, storks, pelicans, and green turtles.

Florida was held at different times by Spain and England until the United States bought it from Spain in 1819. In the early 19th century, Americans were often at war with the Seminoles. These wars did not end until 1842. Florida became a state in 1865. Miami and Jacksonville are two of the largest cities in the state. Tallahassee is the capital.

Florida is a peninsula, which means it is surrounded by water on three sides. Because of this, it has many beaches. Today millions of tourists visit Florida each year. They come to enjoy the warm sunshine and beautiful beaches, as well as amusement parks such as

Miami has more people than any other city in Florida. It is located at the state's far southeastern tip. In fact, it's closer to Cuba than it is to Florida's capital, Tallahassee.

Walt Disney World and Universal Studios in Orlando. They also visit the Kennedy Space Center in Cape Canaveral and Everglades National Park, where they can see many of the same kinds of amazing animals that Ponce de Leon saw centuries ago.

Kennedy Space Center in Cape Canaveral is the home of NASA's Space Shuttle program and is NASA's launch headquarters.

Venice, Florida, is known as the shark tooth capital of the world. Collecting prehistoric shark teeth there is a favorite pastime for visitors and residents.

Underwater Cows?

Manatees, which look a lot like walruses, are also called sea cows. These strange-looking creatures are found in Florida waters. Adult manatees can grow to be 12 feet long and weigh up to 3,500 pounds. That's as much as seven pianos!

Georgia

Mention the peach state, and most everyone knows you mean Georgia. It is the largest state in the south, and the largest state east of the Mississippi River. From the Appalachian Mountains in the north to the Okefenokee Swamp in the south, Georgia is a land of great beauty. In colonial times, forests and woodlands covered most of Georgia, and 66 percent of it remains that way today.

In 1733, James Oglethorpe and a group of poor settlers from England arrived and named this colony Georgia, after King George of England. Georgia became the fourth state on January 2, 1788. During the Civil War, many battles were fought there. General Sherman set fire to Atlanta and burned the city to the ground. It was rebuilt with Southern perseverance and grit, and today the large capital city of modern-day Georgia hustles and bustles.

For many years, most people in Georgia grew cotton. But later they began to grow other crops, and Georgia is now what you might call the "p" state. That's because it is the top producing state for peaches, peanuts, and pecans. It is also the birthplace (and current home) of one U.S. president. Jimmy Carter was born in the small town of Plains, Georgia.

One of the country's most unique landmarks is in Georgia: Stone Mountain, the world's largest sculpture. Carved into the face of the mountain are the figures of three Confederate heroes: Stonewall Jackson, Jefferson Davis, and Robert E. Lee. Lee's horse, Traveler, is also featured.

The carving on the Stone Mountain was conceived in 1909 by Helen Plane.

Georgia's Gold Rush

The first gold rush in North America didn't take place in the Wild West or in Alaska. It took place in Georgia. That's why Georgia's capitol has a gold dome. The gold was mined from Dahlonega, Georgia, where the gold rush started.

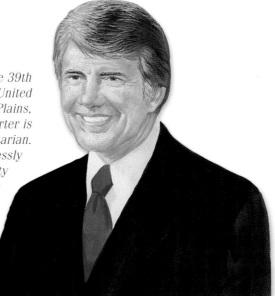

Jimmy Carter, the 39th president of the United States, was born in Plains, Georgia. Today Carter is renowned as a humanitarian. He has worked tirelessly for Habitat for Humanity since 1984 and won the Nobel Peace Prize in 2002. The Jimmy Carter Presidential Library & Museum is located in Atlanta.

Hawaii

Today only two volcanoes in Hawaii are still active. Kilauea, on the Big Island of Hawaii, began spewing lava regularly in 1983, and since that time the island has grown 500 acres larger. The other active volcano is Mauna Loa, also located on the island of Hawaii.

The state of Hawaii is made up of 132 islands. These islands are actually the tips of mountains that rise from the ocean floor. These mountains were formed by volcanoes more than 70 million years ago.

The very first Hawaiians came there from other islands. They named the islands after Hawaii Loa, the chief who led them there; then the islands were divided among many chiefs. In 1795, all the islands were controlled by King Kamehameha I. But as ships from Europe arrived on the islands, many foreigners were given power in the government. In 1891, Queen Liliuokalani became Hawaii's first, and only, queen. She tried, unsuccessfully, to put native Hawaiians back into the government. By this time, Americans were running the islands. In 1900, Hawaii became a U.S. territory. On August 21, 1959, Hawaii became the 50th state. The 1,250,000 or so people who live in Hawaii today come from more than 50 ethnic groups.

On December 7, 1941, the Japanese attacked the U.S. naval base at Pearl Harbor. The next day the United States entered World War II. Today, this memorial in the harbor honors those who died in the attack.

Idaho

The Potato State

More potatoes are grown in Idaho than in any other state. But the first potatoes came from South America. Spanish explorers who visited South America took potatoes back to Europe with them. People who came to settle in the American colonies brought potatoes with them. Many of these people eventually settled in Idaho, and the potato found a home too.

Idaho is a beautiful state. About 80 percent of the northern part of the state is forests, while the southern part has more farmland. The state also has more than 2,000 lakes and more than 16,000 miles of rivers and streams.

Long ago, many Native American nations, such as the Nez Percé, Shoshone, and Coeur d'Alene, made their homes in Idaho. But most were eventually forced out by soldiers.

The first group of white people to visit Idaho was the Lewis and Clark expedition in 1805. Soon after that, traders and trappers came to the area, too. When gold was discovered during the 1860s, thousands of miners moved to Idaho seeking their fortune. In 1890, Idaho became the 43rd state.

Chief Joseph, the great Native American leader of the Nez Percé, was leading his people to Canada in 1877. Many died on their three-month trek. U.S. troops surrounded the Nez Percé in Idaho about 30 miles from the Canadian border. In surrender, Chief Joseph told his soldiers: "I am tired; my heart is sick and sad. From where the sun now stands, I will fight no more forever."

Illinois

The land now known as Illinois was first inhabited by Native Americans who called themselves *Illini* or *Illiniwek*. Back then, the area was mostly treeless plains covered in tall, thick prairie grasses. When French settlers came to this area in the late 1600s, they named it Illinois.

Illinois became the 21st state in December 1818. At that time, Chicago was only a small trading post. Today it is the largest city in the state and the third largest in the country. Almost 12.5 million people live in Illinois, and more than half of them live in or near Chicago. The city also draws many tourists who come to visit such attractions as the Sears Tower, the world-class museums, and the lakefront parks.

Although Illinois is still called the Prairie State, there isn't much prairie left today. But the soil there is very rich, and much of the land is used for growing crops such as corn and soybeans.

The Sears Tower, built in Chicago in 1973, has 110 stories. It is the tallest building in the United States and one of the five tallest in the world.

Land of Lincoln

Abraham Lincoln, the country's 16th president, lived and worked most of his life in Illinois. He was a lawyer in Springfield, the state capital, when he was elected president in 1860.

Indiana

This state lies in the middle of the Midwest, so it is called the Crossroads of America. As early settlers crossed through Indiana on their way out west, some decided to stay there and make it their home. They knew they could farm the rich soil to make a living.

The name *Indiana* means "land of the Indians," but as more white settlers moved into the Indiana Territory, they pushed the Native Americans farther west. Today, fewer than 8,000 Native Americans live in Indiana.

Indiana became a state in 1816. In the years before the Civil War, Fountain City, Indiana, was known as "the Grand Central Station of the Underground Railroad." More than 2,000 runaway slaves stopped there on their way north to freedom.

Many steel mills, oil refineries, and factories were built in Indiana during the 1800s. In the 1900s, Indiana faced tough times. Many farms failed, factories closed, and people lost their jobs. State leaders have worked hard to attract new businesses and industries, and Indiana is once again a thriving part of the country.

The Indianapolis 500 is held every Memorial Day weekend in Indiana's capital city. This legendary race, "The Greatest Spectacle in Racing," is 500 miles long—that's 200 laps around Indianapolis Motor Speedway.

Iowa

Paradise for Rock Hounds

A rock hound is someone who collects rocks. Iowa is a great place for rock hounds because they can find beautiful geodes (Iowa's state rock) in the limestone there. A geode looks like a regular rock on the outside, but the inside is lined with shiny crystals.

Native American nations, including the Iowa, Ottawa, Illinois, and Sioux, were the first people to live in what is now Iowa. They built their homes near two great rivers—the Mississippi and the Missouri. In the 1800s, white settlers forced these Native Americans from their land, claiming it for themselves. They did as the Native Americans had done, settling along the rivers. Many of Iowa's present-day big cities—Des Moines, Sioux City, and Dubuque—are by rivers.

Because Iowa has rich farmland, many of the people who settled there long ago were farmers. Farming is still one of the most important industries in Iowa. The state leads the country in the production of corn, which

Des Moines, the capital of Iowa and Iowa's largest city, sits on the banks of the Des Moines River.

is used as food for both people and animals. Farmers in Iowa also raise hogs, cattle, sheep, turkeys, and horses.

Kansas

Did you know that the exact middle of the continental United States is in Kansas? The spot is marked by a stone podium near Lebanon, Kansas.

The first people to live in Kansas were the Kansas, Osage, Pawnee, and Wichita nations. Eventually, Spanish and French explorers came to the area, and in the

Kansas leads the nation in wheat production. The state is called the Breadbasket of America.

1850s many white settlers made their homes there. Back then, the country was divided over the question of slavery. The northern states did not believe in slavery. The southern states did. Before Kansas became a state, there was a lot of fighting over the issue. Finally, Kansas became part of the Union in 1861 as a state that did not allow slavery.

When early settlers came to Kansas, they had to cut down much of the prairie grass in order to grow crops. Life on the prairie was tough. Many people lived in sod houses that were built partially underground, and it was common to see grass growing on the roofs. These homes usually had a single room with a dirt floor, and "chips" of dried manure were used to heat them in the winter.

Kentucky

Ancient Indians were the first to live in what is now Kentucky. This area contains thick forests and large mountains, which made it difficult for American colonists in the 1700s who wanted to move west. They needed to find a way to cross the mountains in eastern Kentucky. Finally, a man named Thomas Walker discovered a mountain pass, which he called the Cumberland Gap.

Daniel Boone and his woodsmen cleared a trail to the West called the Wilderness Road, and then they led many settlers into Kentucky. People liked this area because of its rich farmland, grasslands, and coal deposits.

Kentucky is called the Bluegrass State because the nickname describes the color of the Kentucky landscape. But there's another reason: Bluegrass music got its start in Kentucky. This type of music includes mandolins, fiddles, guitars, and banjos.

The Kentucky Derby in Louisville is the oldest horse race in the United States.

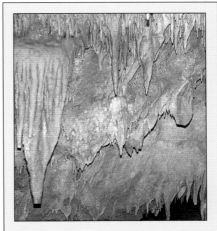

An Underground World

The Mammoth Cave system in Kentucky is the longest system of caves in the world. It has five levels and more than 340 miles of passageways. Visitors can see rocks shaped like trees and flowers and others that are brightly colored. This cave system is actually an underground world with lakes, rivers, waterfalls, and more than 200 species of animals.

Louisiana

Louisiana is a boot-shape state in the southern United States on the Gulf of Mexico. Much of the area is made up of woods and wetlands with many swamps, marshes, bayous, and lakes. The climate there is hot and humid most of the time.

In 1803, the United States bought a large area of land from France for $15 million. This land included Louisiana and parts of 13 other states and was called the Louisiana Purchase. The purchase doubled the size of the country.

Cajuns are a group of people who live in southern Louisiana today. Because their ancestors came from Acadia (a 17th-century French colony on the northeast coast of Canada), they are called Acadians, or Cajuns. The Cajun language, culture, and special way of cooking are all alive in Louisiana today, particularly in New Orleans. A huge Mardi Gras celebration takes place in New Orleans every February.

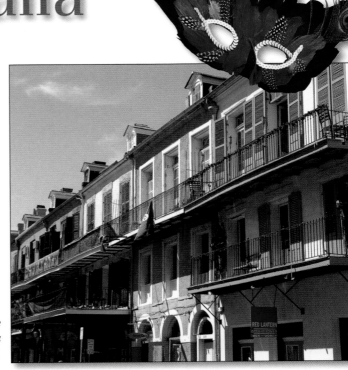

New Orleans was one of the world's busiest ports until it was hit by Hurricane Katrina in 2005.

Maine

The Toothpick Capital

Maine is known as the toothpick capital of the world because about 90 percent of the country's toothpick supply is produced there.

Lighthouses can be seen all along the coast of Maine. The Portland Head Light at Cape Elizabeth is one of the oldest lighthouses in America. It was built in 1791.

Maine is called the Pine Tree State because much of the land there is covered in forests. It's not surprising that the state has many sawmills and lumber camps, and all kinds of wood products are manufactured there. In fact, timber is one of Maine's most important industries.

Maine is located on the Atlantic Coast, and it is noted for its picturesque fishing villages, historic lighthouses, and delicious lobster (which is shipped all over the world). Every year thousands of tourists visit Maine to enjoy its beautiful beaches and winter ski resorts and to see the fantastic display of fall foliage during the autumn months.

Even though Mainers fought for the colonial army in the Revolutionary War, Maine did not become a state until 1820. It joined the Union as a free state, which, at that time, kept the numbers of free states and slave states equal.

Augusta is the capital of Maine, but Portland is its largest city. Today, about 1.3 million people live in this charming state in the northeast corner of the country.

Maryland

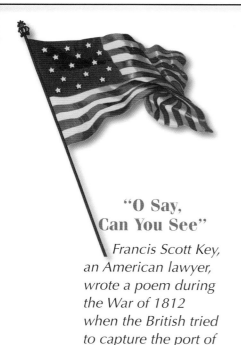

"O Say, Can You See"

Francis Scott Key, an American lawyer, wrote a poem during the War of 1812 when the British tried to capture the port of Baltimore and Fort McHenry. The poem later became the words to the national anthem "The Star-Spangled Banner."

Maryland is unusual in that it has a large body of water, called the Chesapeake Bay, running right through the middle of it. In fact, it almost cuts the state in half. The Cheasapeake Bay is the largest estuary (a place where saltwater and freshwater meet) in the United States. For centuries, people have enjoyed this part of the country. Even as far back as 1608, Captain John Smith thought there was "no place more perfect for man's habitation" than the Chesapeake Bay.

Maryland was founded as a colony where people of different religious beliefs could practice their various faiths. During the Revolutionary War, people in Maryland built ships and cannons for the colonial army. The Maryland State House of Annapolis was the site for the signing of the Treaty of Paris, in 1784,

The Chesapeake and Delaware Canal connects the Delaware River with the Chesapeake Bay and the port of Baltimore.

which ended the Revolutionary War. In 1788, Maryland became the seventh state.

Today, more than five million people live in Maryland. Many work for the federal government in nearby Washington, D.C. Baltimore is the largest city in the state, and Annapolis is the capital.

Massachusetts

When European explorers first came to what is now Massachusetts, Algonquian Native Americans were already living there. In the 1600s, two groups of people from England set sail for America in search of religious freedom. The first group, the Pilgrims, sailed on a ship called the *Mayflower*. In 1620, the Pilgrims created Plymouth Colony in the southwestern part of what is now Massachusetts. They celebrated the first Thanksgiving one year later. The other group that settled in Massachusetts was called the Puritans. In 1630, they formed a settlement called the Massachusetts Bay Colony near present-day Boston.

In 1692, many people in Salem, Massachusetts, were accused of being witches and were forced to stand trial. If convicted of being a witch, they were sentenced to death. Nineteen people were hanged before the trials ended in January 1693. More than 550 original court documents pertaining to these trials are stored at the Peabody Essex Museum in Salem.

On the night of April 18, 1775, Paul Revere made his famous "midnight ride" through Lexington and Concord to warn the militias that the British troops were coming. This night marked the beginning of the Revolutionary War. When the war ended, Massachusetts became the sixth state of the new nation.

The soil in Massachusetts is too thin and rocky for farming. However, about a third of the nation's cranberries are grown here in wet, spongy soil called bogs. During the Civil War, World War I, and World War II, Massachusetts factory workers made ships and weapons. Today, factories in Massachusetts produce scientific instruments, books, newspapers, and electrical equipment. Massachusetts is also a leading fishing state: Fishers catch cod, flounder, scallops, clams, crabs, and lobster off the coast. Tourism is an important part of commerce there, too. Tourists vacation on Cape Cod, visit historic sites throughout the state, and spend time in the Berkshire Hills.

Boston's historic Beacon Hill area offers a peek at what a 19th-century neighborhood must have looked like.

A flooded cranberry bog filled with berries waits to be harvested.

The USS Constitution, *better known as "Old Ironsides," is a stop on Boston's historic Freedom Trail.*

Hoop Dreams

James Naismith just wanted to create a team sport that could be played indoors, out of the cold, when he nailed two peach baskets to a railing in a gym one snowy winter day in Springfield, Massachusetts. He gave the players a large ball, made up 13 rules, and the game of basketball was born.

Michigan

Michigan has lots of shoreline to provide some very pretty scenery.

What state is shaped like a mitten? Why, that's Michigan. In fact, people who live here use the palm of their hand to show locations in the state. But only part of Michigan is shaped that way. The state has two parts, which are separated by water. The northern part of Michigan is called the Upper Peninsula. The part that's shaped like a mitten is called the Lower Peninsula. Michigan is nicknamed the Great Lakes State because Lakes Erie, Huron, Michigan, and Superior touch Michigan. Lake Ontario is the only Great Lake that does not touch the state at all.

French fur traders came to Michigan in the 1600s, but there were few settlers until 1825, when the Erie Canal opened. The canal linked the eastern states to the western territories, and more people came to settle in Michigan.

In the late 1800s, many automobile factories were built in Detroit. The city became known as the Motor City. Thousands of people found jobs at these factories. Automobiles are still produced in Michigan today. But the state also produces iron and copper; and crops like grains, fruits, and vegetables are grown there, too.

Cereal Bowl of America

The city of Battle Creek is the birthplace of two world-famous cereal companies: Kellogg's and Post. Today, more breakfast cereal is produced in Battle Creek than in any other city in the world.

Minnesota

If you enjoy cold weather, you'd probably like Minnesota. The town of International Falls is known as the coldest place in the United States. The state has plenty of ice and snow, so winter sports such as skiing, sledding, and riding snowmobiles are popular there. But summer sports including fishing, waterskiing, and canoeing are enjoyed by thousands of people there, too.

Minnesota has miles of pine forests near its northern border, which touches Canada. About two million Christmas trees come from Minnesota each year. Southern Minnesota has very rich farmland, where sugar beets grow and dairy cows graze. Minnesota also leads the nation in iron ore production.

The mighty Mississippi is the nation's biggest and longest river. It begins at Lake Itasca in Minnesota, where it is just inches deep and a few feet wide. In fact, you can easily wade across it there!

The city of Minneapolis has reclaimed the river front fo.

The two largest cities in Minnesota are St. Paul (the capital) and Minneapolis. These two cities are right across the Mississippi River from each other. They are called the twin cities, although they aren't much alike.

Even though Minnesota has more than 15,000 lakes, one of its nicknames is Land of 10,000 Lakes. It has 90,000 miles of shoreline. That's more than California, Florida, and Hawaii combined.

Mississippi

In the early 1800s, Mississippi was truly "the land of cotton." White plantation owners became very wealthy growing cotton, because they bought African slaves to work in the cotton fields. At that time, Mississippi's economy relied on slavery. It was the second state to secede (or leave) the Union and join the Confederacy during the Civil War.

After the Civil War, slaves were freed and given the right to vote and hold office. However, African-Americans were still not treated equally. Laws were made in Mississippi that segregated (separated) whites and African-Americans. In the 1960s, African-Americans were tired of being denied their civil rights. Many civil rights marches were held in the state, and in 1969, a federal court ordered that schools could no longer be separated by race. This was one of the first efforts to end segregation in Mississippi. Today, residents of all races work together to improve their state.

Mississippi has a rich cultural history: American music traditions such as gospel, jazz, blues, and rock 'n' roll developed there.

Today, cotton is still an important crop. Almost two million acres of cotton are planted in Mississippi.

A Cactus in Mississippi?

You probably don't think of cacti when you think of this state, but the world's largest cactus plantation is in Edwards, Mississippi.

Missouri

Missouri is located in the center of the United States. Two great rivers run through the state—the Missouri and the Mississippi. Naturally, they helped make the state a top transportation center.

Lewis and Clark started their journey to explore the Northwest in Missouri, near St. Louis on the Missouri River. Eventually this area became known as the Gateway to the West. Both the Santa Fe and Oregon trails started in Missouri. Today the Gateway Arch in St. Louis reminds everyone of Missouri's rich history as the starting point for those who traveled west so long ago.

The Gateway Arch is the tallest monument in the United States.

The Missouri Compromise

Before Missouri became a state, efforts were made to ban slavery there. However, in 1821, Missouri entered the Union as a slave state as part of the Missouri Compromise. This compromise was created to maintain a balance of power in Congress. According to the compromise, Maine was admitted into the Union as a free state, and Missouri was admitted as a slave state, which kept the number of free states and slave states equal.

Montana

The Rocky Mountains tower over much of western Montana. The name Montana comes from the Spanish word *montaña*, which means "mountain." The state is sometimes called the Big Sky Country. The eastern three-fifths of Montana is Great Plains, so the sky seems endless over these wide prairie lands. Large farms and ranches cover this area.

In fact, "big" is a good word to describe this state overall. Montana is the fourth largest state. It's so big that the entire country of England would fit inside it three times!

Did you know the Crown Jewels of England include a gem from North America? The Montana Yogo Sapphire is the only North American gem that has that distinction. Yogo sapphires are more rare than diamonds and are among the finest natural sapphires in the world.

Gold was discovered in Montana in 1862, and many people flocked to the region seeking fortune. In 1888, it was home to 50 millionaires. Today, Montana has more gem sapphires than any other state and is an important source of gold, silver, copper, and lead.

While the state of Montana is large, its population is small. There are only five people per square mile. However, it has a large population of Native Americans, with seven American Indian reservations in the state.

More people visit Glacier National Park than any other spot in the state.

Nebraska

The Pawnee people were the first residents of Nebraska. They lived near the North Platte River for many years, hunting buffalo and raising corn and beans for food. But in 1854, the U.S. Government opened up the Nebraska Territory for settlement. Suddenly, thousands of pioneers settled there and built towns, farms, and ranches. The Native Americans fought bravely to keep their land, but eventually they were forced to move to reservations.

The state tree of Nebraska is the cottonwood, which grows best in moist soil. Years ago, this tree was helpful to settlers coming to the region. They knew that wherever they saw the cottonwoods was a good place to build because it meant water was nearby.

Life wasn't easy for the settlers who came to Nebraska in the 1800s. Grasshoppers, blizzards, dust storms, and lack of water made farming difficult. But when Nebraska became a state in 1867, the government helped farmers build irrigation systems to water their crops. Today, farms and ranches cover 95 percent of the state.

Many of the people in Nebraska live near urban areas, such as Omaha (the state's largest city) and Lincoln (the capital).

Corn is one of the leading farm products in Nebraska.

Lake Tahoe is one of the deepest, largest, and highest lakes in the country. Only Crater Lake in Oregon is deeper.

Nevada

Nevada has a unique geography: It is mostly covered by mountains and desert. The name Nevada comes from a Spanish word meaning "snow-capped." Much of the state is located within an area called the Great Basin, which is a huge desert that covers parts of six states. Since so much of the state is covered by desert, it shouldn't be surprising that Nevada has only about seven inches of rainfall each year—that's the least amount of any state. Most of the land in Nevada is too dry and salty to farm without irrigation.

Many tales of the Old West happened in Nevada. In 1859, a rich silver deposit was discovered near what is now Virginia City, Nevada. This attracted people from all over who hoped to strike it rich in the silver mines. They set up rough, rowdy mining camps. When the price of silver fell in 1880, the camps were deserted and became ghost towns. Today tourists enjoy visiting the old mining towns in this state.

Mining is still an important industry in Nevada. It is the leading state in production of gold and silver. Today, tourism is the state's biggest industry. Many people go to Las Vegas and Reno to gamble and to see famous entertainers perform on stage. About 32 million people visit Las Vegas each year. Luckily, Vegas is built to entertain—to spend one night in every hotel room in the city would take you more than 288 years!

People also visit Hoover Dam outside of Las Vegas. Visitors can tour the massive dam and enjoy a museum full of artifacts relating to the construction and benefits of the dam.

Lake Tahoe is another popular tourist spot in Nevada. Located in the Sierra Nevada mountains, Lake Tahoe has beautiful ski resorts. In summer, the lake is popular for water sports and beach activities.

Miniature replicas of some of the most famous attractions in Paris, France, can be found in Las Vegas. Here we see the Eiffel Tower and the Arc de Triomphe.

That's a Lot of Concrete!

Hoover Dam outside of Las Vegas contains 3.25 million cubic yards of concrete. That's enough to pave a two-lane highway from San Francisco to New York City.

A Mohave yucca plant in the Red Rock Canyon Conservation Area.

New Hampshire

The community of Wolfeboro is on Lake Winnipesuakee. It is known as "the Oldest Summer Resort in America." At its deepest point, the lake is 213 feet deep.

This state in New England was the third of the original 13 colonies. In 1776, New Hampshire became the first colony to have its own local constitution. Then, in 1788, nine states needed to approve the United States Constitution before it could become law. New Hampshire was the ninth state to do so—and the Constitution became law.

New Hampshire is known for its motto, "Live Free or Die," which originated with Revolutionary War General John Stark. Today, the motto is on the state's license plates.

The Primary Election

Since 1920, New Hampshire has held the first presidential primary in the country. The primaries in states help determine who will run for president. The person who wins New Hampshire's primary often becomes the president of the United States.

The landscape of New Hampshire is beautiful, and it has a lot to offer people who enjoy the outdoors. In the fall, visitors come to admire the leaves of the trees as they turn bright, fiery colors. In winter, skiing is popular in the White Mountains. And in summer, people crowd the lakes and ocean beaches of New Hampshire.

New Jersey

The Trump Taj Mahal is a popular hotel and casino resort in Atlantic City, New Jersey.

Long ago, the Lenape people lived in what is now New Jersey. They farmed, hunted, and fished, traveling along the rivers in canoes made from logs. Then, in the 1600s, Dutch and Swedish fur traders came to this region. Later, the English arrived and gave the area its name, after the English island of Jersey.

In 1787, New Jersey became the third state. Cities, bridges, roads, and railroads were built, connecting the state with other states. Textiles, iron, and steel were produced in factories there, and it became one of the great industrial states. Immigrants poured into New Jersey, hoping to find work and a better life.

Among the major crops of New Jersey are cranberries and blueberries. This state also produces large amounts of peppers, peaches, and tomatoes.

Most people who live in New Jersey today live in or near big cities. To get away, they vacation on Jersey beaches and swim, fish, and sail. Atlantic City, with its famous boardwalk that stretches along the beach, is the state's most popular resort.

The state has other areas covered with rich, rolling hills that are good for crops. More than 17 percent of the state is farmland.

New Mexico

Natural wonders abound in New Mexico. The Rocky Mountains rise in the northern part of the state, and the hot Chihuahuan desert is found in the south. In between, there's everything from fertile valleys and green grasslands to white-sand deserts, rugged red mountains, and deep caves.

People have lived in what is now New Mexico for at least 10,000 years. The first inhabitants were Native Americans: The Mogollon, Anasazi, Pueblo, Navajo, and Apache people have all called this region home. Spain and Mexico also played big roles in New Mexico's history. Spanish explorers arrived in the 1500s, conquering American Indian villages and claiming land for Spain. The explorers were followed by settlers and priests who forced the Native Americans to work for them and converted them to Christianity. There were many uprisings during this time. In 1821, Mexico broke free of Spain's rule. In 1848, the territory of

New Mexico became part of the United States, and in 1912, it became a state.

In the 1880s, railroads in New Mexico brought more people and more trade routes to the state. This spurred a cattle boom. Cattle, dairy products, pecans, chili peppers, and pinto beans are all produced in New Mexico today. There are also research facilities for solar energy, atomic power, and space travel in New Mexico.

The Native American vase on the left is from Taos Pueblo. The buildings above also typify the Native American culture found in Taos, New Mexico.

In the early 1900s, many artists settled in Taos and Santa Fe, because the state had become well known for its diverse culture. Today, Native Americans, Hispanic, and Anglo influences exist throughout New Mexico. It is also a popular tourist spot. People come to see the ancient ruins and beautiful landscapes including White Sands National Monument in southern New Mexico—the world's largest gypsum sand dune field. They also tour the fascinating Carlsbad Caverns, which is home to more than 300,000 bats!

A black bear cub was found burned in a scorched pine tree after a New Mexico forest fire in 1950. A few years earlier, a cartoon bear named Smokey had starred in a fire prevention program. This little bear cub became the real-life Smokey Bear, and the fire prevention program became a huge success.

Four Corners

Want to be in four states at once? Visit the northwest corner of New Mexico where it meets the corners of Arizona, Utah, and Colorado. There you can put your hands and feet in four different states at once!

Carlsbad Caverns has one of the world's largest underground chambers, featuring some of the most spectacular limestone formations, such as these stalactites.

New York

Some eight million people live in New York City, ranking fifth in the world after Tokyo, Japan; Sao Paulo, Brazil; Mexico City, Mexico; and Seoul, South Korea.

New York is the name of both a city and a state. When people envision the city, they think of the towering skyscrapers in Manhattan. But most of New York state is covered by gorgeous lakes, forests, rivers, and mountains. Apple orchards and dairy farms stretch across western New York.

The Adirondack Mountains draw tourists from all over the country. Adirondack Park is larger than Yellowstone, Yosemite, Grand Canyon, Glacier, and Olympic national parks combined! But one of the biggest tourist attractions is Niagara Falls. These enormous falls are on the Niagara River between Lake Ontario and Lake Erie. They are a major source of electricity, producing water power for the state of New York.

In 1609, Henry Hudson claimed the land we now call New York for the Dutch. Back then, the Dutch called it New Netherland. When the British took over the colony in 1664, they renamed it New York after the Duke of York. From 1785 to 1790, New York City was the capital of the United States. In 1788, New York became the 11th state.

In 1886, the Statue of Liberty, a gift from the people of France, was placed on an island in New York Harbor. When immigrants sailed into the harbor, they were welcomed by the dignified statue. The statue's official name is "Liberty Enlightening the World." Immigrants from Europe passed through the immigration building (shown above) on Ellis Island in New York Harbor.

In 1825, the Erie Canal was completed, connecting the city of Albany on the Hudson River to the city of Buffalo on Lake Erie. Soon towns sprang up along the canal in western and central New York. Roads and railroads were built across the state, too. Millions of immigrants arrived in New York, and for awhile it had more people than any other state. Manufacturing, trade, and finance were big businesses in New York, and New York City became the world's busiest port.

Although New York is no longer the top state in population or manufacturing, New York City leads the nation in finance, fashion, and the arts and entertainment. It is a destination for tourists from around the world.

The Niagara River connects Lake Erie to Lake Ontario. Niagara Falls is the name of a group of waterfalls that is part of this river. This view is of American Falls, which is one of these waterfalls.

The State What?

Not every state has a state muffin. But New York does! In 1987, the governor of New York signed a bill that made the apple muffin the official state muffin. Students at an elementary school in North Syracuse asked him to honor their favorite muffin, so he did.

The Herbert C. Bonner Bridge crosses over the Oregon Inlet, the home of the largest and most modern fishing fleet on the eastern seaboard.

North Carolina

Clingman's Dome overlooks Smoky Mountains National Park—a gorgeous view, especially during sunset.

The state of North Carolina is divided into three parts by the land and the culture. The eastern part reminds people of its rich colonial history. Many swamps and fertile farms can be found in this part of the state. Farmers grow tobacco, soybeans, and cotton on the rich coastal plains. The Outer Banks lie off the coast of North Carolina. To get to them, you must cross a long bridge from the mainland.

The central part of the state is where most of the people in North Carolina live. People call it the heart of the state, since many industries are located there. Textiles and furniture making were once the strongest industries in North Carolina, but now technology, research, and banking are growing quickly in this region. Both Raleigh, the state capital, and Charlotte, the largest city, are in central North Carolina.

The western part of the state has the rugged Blue Ridge Mountains and the Smoky Mountains. The area is isolated, yet it is very beautiful.

One nickname for North Dakota is the Flickertail State, which refers to the Richardson ground squirrels that are commonly seen there.

North Dakota

North Dakota is the geographical center of North America. Native Americans were the first to live in North Dakota. The state's name, which means "friend," comes from the Lakota. In 1682, the French claimed the land there, but it was sold to the United States as part of the Louisiana Purchase in 1803. Back then, two explorers, Meriwether Lewis and William Clark, were sent to check out this new territory.

The area was settled slowly because traveling there was difficult, and there were many fights with the Native Americans who lived there. In the 1880s, railroads improved travel, bringing more companies and people to North Dakota. In 1889, Congress divided the Dakota territory into North and South Dakota, and they became the 39th and 40th states.

The state has rolling hills and rich soil for farming. Wheat is the most important crop—it's grown in every county in the state. Barley, soybeans, and sunflowers are other important crops. Farms in the fertile Red River Valley in the east are perfect for growing sugar beets, soybeans, and corn.

The Badlands may have a menacing-sounding name, but they are actually a beautiful place. This area is a valley in western North and South Dakota. Over millions of years, the colorful sandstone and shale have been sculpted by wind and water into strange shapes.

Ohio

The other 49 states have flags that are shaped like a rectangle. But the Ohio state flag has a different shape, and it's called a burgee. A burgee looks like a pennant.

Buckeye trees once grew all over Ohio, so the state is called the Buckeye State. Native Americans thought the dark brown nuts with a tan spot in the center looked like the eye of a buck, or male deer, so they called them "buckeyes." When the first settlers came to Ohio, they cut down most of the buckeye trees to clear the land for farming and to use the wood for log cabins.

The state of Ohio is named for the Ohio River, which forms all of its southern border. The Iroquois called this river *O-hy-o*, which means "good river."

Many of Ohio's first residents came from eastern states in search of good, cheap farmland. In the 1800s, people from other countries began arriving in Ohio. Germans, Welsh, and Irish all found jobs there. African-Americans came to Ohio, too. Many were runaway slaves from the South who escaped to Ohio to live free.

Today, most Ohio residents live in cities. Ohio is known for producing manufactured goods including rubber products, metal products, steel, and machinery. Farmers in the state grow soybeans, corn, and tomatoes and raise hogs, cattle, and poultry.

The Ohio buckeye (left) is poisonous to humans but not to squirrels. It grows from medium-size, deciduous trees like the one above.

The people of Cleveland have wisely invested a lot of money into making the city's skyline a must-see attraction for tourists.

Rock and Roll Hall of Fame

Cleveland has a special place in the history of rock music. In 1951, a Cleveland disc jockey made up the term "rock and roll." And, in 1952, the city hosted the first rock concert, called the Moondog Coronation Ball. So it seems only natural that the Rock and Roll Hall of Fame and Museum was built in Cleveland. At this museum you won't find paintings, fossils, or science exhibits. Instead, you'll learn about the history of rock music as you listen to music, watch concert videos, and look at all sorts of guitars, records, and even concert outfits worn by many rock and roll stars.

Oklahoma

Oklahoma lies at the heart of Tornado Alley, a stretch of land across the middle of the United States. The area is prone to severe thunderstorms because cold air from the Rockies blows east, colliding with warm air masses. The difference in air temperature causes dangerous storms that can sometimes produce tornadoes.

Oklahoma became home to the Choctaw, Cherokee, Creek, Chickawaw, and Seminole nations in the 1830s. These people were forced to give up their lands because the settlers in the east wanted more space. They forced the Native Americans to move west to Oklahoma. Many of them died on this brutal journey.

After the Civil War, railroads were built through this territory, and cattle ranchers from Texas drove their herds through on their way to Kansas. It wasn't long before settlers wanted to live in this part of the country, too. Many of the Native Americans remaining in the territory were forced onto reservations, and their land was given to the settlers.

Oklahoma has the largest Native American population of any state today. About 250,000 Native Americans live there, and it is the tribal headquarters for 39 tribes.

The Wichita Mountains offer some beautiful views of Lake Lawtonka in the middle of Oklahoma.

Oregon

Behind Portland, Oregon, stands the snow-covered, majestic Mount Hood.

Oregon is a beautiful state in the Pacific Northwest. It has splendid, snow-covered mountain peaks, scenic coastlines, and lush valleys. The Cascade Mountains run north to south through the state and divide it into two climate zones. West of the Cascades, the region has a mild climate with heavy rainfall. It's a good area for growing timber trees and flowers. East of the Cascades, the region has hot summers and cold, sunny winters. The southeastern part of the state gets little rain and is very dry.

When explorers first came to the Pacific Northwest in the 1500s, the Chinook, Nez Percé, and Klamath people lived there. Later, in the 1840s and 1850s, many pioneers followed the Oregon Trail to make Oregon their home. In 1848, Oregon became a territory; in 1859, it became a state.

Oregon is one of the fastest growing states today. Many people come to Oregon looking for a beautiful place to live with clean air and good jobs.

A Lake from a Volcano

Crater Lake was formed more than 7,000 years ago when the top of a volcano collapsed, leaving behind a huge crater. Water and rain gradually filled this big hole. Crater Lake is the deepest lake in the country.

23

Pennsylvania

As this sculpture in Philadelphia's Love Park points out, the city is known as the City of Brotherly Love.

The Liberty Bell was rung to announce the first public reading of the Declaration of Independence. The Liberty Bell is on display in Independence Square in Philadelphia.

Millions of years ago the ocean covered Pennsylvania. Later, the ocean receded and the area became swamplands. Eventually, over a very long time, decaying plants from the swamplands turned into coal and oil deposits. And that's how Pennsylvania came to be the major producer of coal in the United States today.

Pennsylvania also has much natural beauty that was created centuries ago. Glaciers that once covered the area during the Ice Age formed mountains, plateaus, rivers, and waterfalls.

In 1681, King Charles of England gave the area now called Pennsylvania to William Penn. Penn wanted his new colony to provide freedom for people of all faiths to practice any religion they chose. His colony grew, and the area of Pennsylvania came to play an important role in the history of the United States.

In 1761, the British built Fort Pitt, which later became Pittsburgh. The nation's leaders wrote two of the country's most important documents—the Declaration of Independence and the U.S. Constitution—in Philadelphia, Pennsylvania. Also, the Liberty Bell is kept in this city.

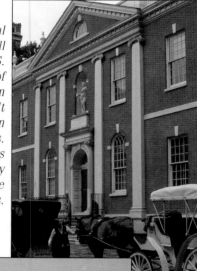

The original Library Hall housed the U.S. Library of Congress from 1774 to 1800. It was demolished in the late 1800s. This replica was built on Library Hall's original site in the 1950s.

This cannon in Gettysburg, Pennsylvania, is a reminder of the Civil War battle.

The Battle of Gettysburg, one of the most famous battles of the Civil War, was fought in Gettysburg, Pennsylvania. Union troops defeated the Confederate troops led by General Robert E. Lee there.

Besides coal, Pennsylvania also produces chemicals, machinery, and farm products such as corn, grapes, oats, peaches, potatoes, wheat, chickens, and dairy products.

Chocolate Town, USA

The world's largest chocolate factory is in Hershey, Pennsylvania. The town was originally named Derry Church but was changed to Hershey when Hershey's chocolate became so popular. Hersheypark is a huge theme park with more than 60 rides.

Rhode Island

Rhode Island, at only 48 miles long and 37 miles wide, is the smallest of the 50 states. You can easily drive across the entire state in an hour! Like William Penn, who founded Pennsylvania, Roger Williams, an English minister in Massachusetts, thought people should be able to worship as they pleased. The Puritans of Massachusetts did not agree with Williams, so he moved away and started his own colony, which became Rhode Island. People of all faiths were welcome there.

Because Rhode Island is on the coast, it was a center for trade and shipping in the 1700s. Later, it became a center of industry. By 1860, it was the most industrialized state in the nation. Today, Rhode Island relies mainly on service industries and tourism.

A State Chicken?

Every state has a state bird, and Rhode Island's state bird is the Rhode Island Red Chicken, a breed developed in the 1850s. This chicken made poultry a major industry in Rhode Island, so it seemed like a good choice for the state bird.

The Castle Hill Lighthouse near Newport, Rhode Island, was built in 1890. The lighthouse is still active and serves as a signal to navigators.

One of the most beautiful areas in Charleston is Battery Park, where people like to walk and take in the sights.

South Carolina

Although the English weren't the first Europeans to try to settle in the South Carolina area, they were the most successful. They built the city of Charleston in 1670 and grew rice and indigo (a plant used to make blue dye) to ship to England. South Carolina soon became a rich colony.

After 1800, cotton was the state's top crop. Plantation owners used slaves to plant and harvest the cotton crops, so naturally the white slave owners in the state did not want slavery abolished. In 1860, South Carolina was the first state to secede (leave) from the Union. After the Civil War, it was a very poor state. After World War II, the economy began to improve. Today, thanks to such industries and products as chemicals, textiles, machinery, lumber, crabs, and shrimp, South Carolina is one of the fastest-growing states in the South.

The first shots of the Civil War were fired at Fort Sumter. Today it's a national monument that you can tour.

25

South Dakota

The Sioux, who lived in this area before white settlers moved there, called it *Dakota,* meaning "friend." South Dakota is a state full of beautiful and varied lands, historic sites, and natural wonders. Farmers raise crops in the prairies in the east, while the Great Plains have big livestock ranches as well as the Badlands, where strange rock formations were carved over many years by wind and water. In the far west of the state are mountains with many evergreen trees. These are called the Black Hills.

The most famous landmark in South Dakota is Mount Rushmore National Memorial in the Black Hills outside Rapid City. The faces of four United States presidents—

More than 2.6 million people visit Mount Rushmore each year. The huge sculpture is chiseled into a granite mountain in South Dakota.

The Crazy Horse Memorial

Did you know there's another enormous memorial in South Dakota, even bigger than Mount Rushmore? Nearby, another sculpture is being carved into a different mountain. The Crazy Horse Memorial depicts this famed Native American leader on his horse. When it is finished, it will be the world's largest sculpture.

George Washington, Thomas Jefferson, Theodore Roosevelt, and Abraham Lincoln— are carved into the side of the mountain. People can also travel to the mining town of Deadwood to see what life was like in the Wild West and visit the spots where Wild Bill Hickok and Calamity Jane are buried.

Tennessee

From 1763 to 1789, Tennessee was part of North Carolina. But mountains separated it from the rest of North Carolina, so it was difficult for people to move into this territory. In 1775, Daniel Boone created a trail through the Cumberland Gap, and settlers began to move to what is now Tennessee.

Before the Civil War, many cotton farmers in western Tennessee owned slaves, while white people in eastern Tennessee were against slavery. The state eventually joined the Confederacy.

Today, farms cover about half of Tennessee. Beef cattle and cotton are the state's two most important farm products.

The Great Smoky Mountains National Park stretches across Tennessee and North Carolina. It is one of the most beautiful parks in the United States.

Home of The King

Elvis Presley was known as the king of rock 'n' roll. Each year, millions of fans visit Graceland, Presley's estate in Memphis. It's the most visited house in the United States besides the White House.

Memphis is Tennessee's largest city, while Nashville is the state capital and second largest city in the state. Nashville is famous for the Grand Ole Opry and country music, while Memphis will always be known for the blues, rock 'n' roll, and Graceland, the home of Elvis Presley.

Texas

Texas is called the Lone Star State, and a single star appears on the state flag. But since the 1500s, six flags have flown over Texas. Texas has been part of Spain, France, Mexico, the Confederacy, and the United States. For nearly ten years it was also an independent republic.

Texas is a big state. Only Alaska is larger. Austin is the state capital, and Houston is its largest city. More than 20 million people live in Texas. Overall, only California has a larger population. About one of every three Texans is Latino.

In the early 1900s, oil was discovered in many places throughout Texas. Oil fields and refineries were built, and people came from all around to work in them. In 1902, 17.5 million barrels of oil were pumped out of Spindletop Hill, Texas. Around that time things started to change in Texas, and the state's economy was dependent on the oil industry for many years. Today Texas doesn't depend on oil as much as it once did.

Remember the Alamo!

The Alamo in San Antonio is the state's most popular historic site. In 1835, war broke out when American settlers in Texas wanted to be free of Mexican rule. The Mexican Army attacked the Alamo, and the Texans who defended it were killed, including Davy Crockett and Jim Bowie. Later, the Texans defeated the Mexicans, and Texas won its independence from Mexico. Their battle cry was "Remember the Alamo," and today the Alamo is considered the cradle of Texas liberty.

Chemicals, natural gas, and petroleum help support the state's economy. Cattle, shrimp, and cotton are also important products.

Texas is a leading producer of oil. Most drilling takes place in the area known as the Texas Panhandle. The state is also known for its large cattle ranches, which provide much of the country's supply of beef.

Holy Vampires, Batman!

Texas is home to more species of bats than any other state in the country.

27

Utah

The Mormon Temple is located in downtown Salt Lake City's Temple Square. It took 40 years to build.

During the days of the Wild West, many pioneers passed through Utah on their way to a better life out west. But some of the people stayed in Utah and made it their home. Many of those people who stayed were members of the Church of Jesus Christ of Latter-day Saints, more commonly called Mormons. Like many people before them, the Mormons were looking for a place where they could worship as they pleased. In 1847, they settled in an area near the Great Salt Lake. As more people moved to the area, they used irrigation to make the land suitable for farming, and more Mormons, as well as other people, moved to the area.

In 1896, Utah became the 45th state. Today 2.2 million people live in Utah. About 80 percent of them live in or near big cities, including the capital, which is Salt Lake City. The most important product in Utah is oil. The state also produces livestock and food for livestock, such as hay.

The Great Salt Lake is the largest salt lake in the Western Hemisphere, but its size changes each year. In wet years the lake becomes bigger. In dry years the lake becomes smaller. It also gets saltier because there is less water to dilute the salt. Swimmers float more easily in saltwater than freshwater. If you went swimming in the Great Salt Lake during a dry year, you would be almost unsinkable!

Vermont

Vermont is famous for its covered bridges. It has more than 100 of them. The Windsor-Cornish covered bridge, which connects Vermont to New Hampshire, is the longest covered bridge in the country.

Three-quarters of this state is covered with forestland, so it's no wonder that thousands of tourists travel to Vermont each year to admire the beautifully colored autumn leaves on the trees. The locals call these visitors "leaf peepers." People also love the Green Mountains, which run down the center of the state.

After the Revolutionary War, the 13 colonies became the United States. Vermont was not one of those colonies. It became a country of its own and stayed that way for 14 years. In 1791, Vermont became the 14th state, the first one to enter the Union after the original 13 colonies.

Vermonters today love the natural beauty of their state and have passed some of the strictest environmental laws in the country.

Vermont is the biggest producer of maple syrup in the United States. Native Americans were the first to learn how to make maple syrup by boiling tree sap.

Virginia

Virginia is rich in history. In 1607, English colonists started a settlement on the east coast of North America. They named it Jamestown. They called the land Virginia, after Queen Elizabeth. (She was known as the Virgin Queen.) Jamestown, Virginia, was the first permanent English settlement in North America. Because of this, Virginia is known as "the birthplace of a nation."

Today, history is brought to life for tourists in an old-fashioned community called Colonial Williamsburg. This 301-acre historic area has hundreds of restored, reconstructed, and historically furnished buildings. Costumed workers practice old-fashioned trades such as blacksmithing and give visitors a glimpse of what life was like in an 18th-century town.

Visitors to Virginia can also see the homes of some American presidents. Mount Vernon was the home of George Washington. Monticello was Thomas Jefferson's home.

Virginia is a beautiful state with a variety of landscapes. The eastern part of the state is called the Tidewater. It borders the Atlantic Ocean, so it has beaches, bays, and marshes. The Piedmont is the name of the middle of the state. The word means "foot of the mountain." The Blue Ridge and Allegheny Mountains begin there. They are part of the Appalachians, the oldest mountain chain in North America.

Famous historic sites in Virginia include Mount Vernon, George Washington's home, and Colonial Williamsburg, where young people act out the fife-and-drum corps that led Colonial soldiers into battle against the British.

Shenandoah National Park in Virginia stretches along the Blue Ridge Mountains.

Mother Virginia

Virginia has been called the Mother of Presidents. Eight U.S. Presidents were born in Virginia: George Washington, Thomas Jefferson, James Madison, James Monroe, William Henry Harrison, John Tyler, Zachary Taylor, and Woodrow Wilson.

Virgina is also called the Mother of States. All or part of eight other states are made from land that was once part of Virginia.

George Washington

Thomas Jefferson

The Pocahontas Story: Fact or Myth?

In the early 1600s, the Algonquian people captured Jamestown's John Smith. They were about to kill him when the chief's daughter, Pocahontas, threw herself between Smith and the attackers, saving his life. But is this story true, or is it merely a popular myth?

Washington

One of the most familiar sights of Seattle's skyline is the Space Needle. At 605 feet tall, the Space Needle was the tallest building west of the Mississippi River when it was built in 1962.

Mount St. Helens

This volcano is part of the Cascade Mountain Range and is located 95 miles south of Seattle. The last time a major eruption occurred here was on May 18, 1980.

Named after George Washington, this is the only state in the nation named after a U.S. president. The Lewis and Clark expedition followed the Columbia River to the Pacific Northwest in 1805, and fur traders settled in the area in the 1800s. Washington became part of the Oregon Territory in 1848, and in 1889 it became the 42nd state.

Thanks to the Pacific Ocean, the western part of the state has mild seasons and a lot of rain. The eastern part of the state is drier, so farms there have to rely on irrigation for their crops of Washington apples. Apples are big business in Washington. It produces more apples than any other state.

Washington has many mountainous areas. Mount Rainier, one of the nation's highest mountains, is part of the Cascade Mountains. But most of the state's population lives in the Puget Sound Lowland. Around Puget Sound are many of Washington's largest cities, including Seattle.

West Virginia

Shooting the Rapids

If you like to go white-water rafting, West Virginia is the place for you. The Gauley River is one of the best rivers to raft. It has 26 miles of fast-moving water and more than 100 rapids. Rapids named Lost Paddle, Pillow Rock, Iron Ring, and Heaven Help Us offer a combination of natural beauty and white-water fun.

West Virginia is called the Mountain State because the entire state lies within the Appalachian Mountain system. There is very little flat ground in West Virginia, so there aren't many farms in this state. There are no large cities in West Virginia, either. Most people live in rural areas, and many of them are somewhat isolated.

West Virginia used to be part of Virginia. During the Civil War, most people in eastern Virginia supported slavery, while people in western Virginia were against it. When Virginia joined the Confederacy, the people in western Virginia broke away and

West Virginia has many scenic parks, including Babcock State Park. The Glade Creek Grist Mill is located in the park near the New River Gorge.

formed their own state. West Virginia became the 35th state in 1863.

In the 1800s, many men in West Virginia worked in coal mining. It was dirty, dangerous work with long hours and little pay. Today tourism has replaced coal as the state's leading industry.

Wisconsin

Wisconsin is located in the upper Midwest. The area includes beautiful forests, dairy farms, prairies, cliffs, and more than 15,000 lakes. The Menominee, Winnebago, and Dakota nations were among the first to live in Wisconsin. In the 1630s, fur traders began to explore the area, and in the 1820s, settlers came to mine lead. Wisconsin joined the Union in 1848.

The state has rich farmland, but it is now used mostly to raise dairy cows. Wisconsin makes more cheese than any other state and is famous for other dairy products, too. Wisconsin also produces items such as machines, food products, paper, and electrical equipment.

Frank Lloyd Wright was born in Wisconsin. He became one of America's most famous architects. He designed houses that blended with the flat Midwest prairies. The houses were built so low that they seemed to be part of the ground. Wright also used terraces and porches to make the indoors part of the outdoors.

Five million people live in Wisconsin. Milwaukee is the largest city. People of different backgrounds live there and celebrate their diverse cultures.

Wisconsin is so proud of its dairy industry that it named the dairy cow its official domestic animal.

Wyoming

Wyoming takes its name from a Native American phrase that means "at the big plains." The Great Plains cover parts of eastern Wyoming. Near the center of the state they give way to the tall peaks of the Rocky Mountains, which cover much of western Wyoming.

Wyoming is a state with lots of wide-open spaces and few people. With less than half a million people, Wyoming has fewer people than any other state.

Ranching has been important to Wyoming's industry for many years, but today its most important industry is energy. Wyoming is the leading state for coal production and is also a leader in producing petroleum and natural gas.

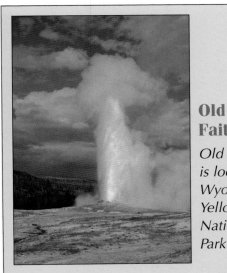

Old Faithful

Old Faithful is located in Wyoming's Yellowstone National Park.

Wyoming has some of the most beautiful, rugged country in the United States, including Grand Teton National Park.

Washington, D.C.

Washington, D.C., is the capital city of the United States. It was named after George Washington. It is the only city in the country that isn't part of a state. Instead, it is in the District of Columbia, and it belongs to the citizens of all the states.

Europeans first arrived in this area in the early 1600s. Native Americans were already living there. A large river with steep banks ran through the area. There were marshes, swamps, lots of trees, and many wild animals. Soon the area was filled with plantations and farms. By 1700, the land had been divided among the new settlers, and few Native Americans remained. In 1790, Congress chose the area to be the country's capital.

Today, Washington, D.C., is rich in historical landmarks, including the White House, home to every United States President since John Adams. The city is one of the most pop-ular tourist spots in the country. People come to see the National Mall, a large open area about a mile long in the center of the city. It includes many monuments and also connects the White House and the United States Capitol. The Washington Monument is located in the center of the Mall. Nearby are the Jefferson Memorial, Lincoln Memorial, and other famous monuments. The city is also home to the world-famous Smithsonian Institution and many fine museums.

The centers of all three branches of the U.S. federal government are located in the District of Columbia. National and international institutions such as the World Bank, the International Monetary Fund, and the Organization of American States are headquartered there.

Although George Washington observed the White House being built, he never lived in it. John Adams, the second president, was the first president to live in the historic building.

Visit the Bureau of Engraving and Printing in Washington, D.C., and you can watch money being printed. Sheets of paper, each one made up of 32 bills, roll off the presses. Just how much money is printed there? The bureau says 37 million bills a day. That's about $696 million!

The Washington Monument was built to honor the first president of the United States. The landmark is just over 555 feet tall and was completed in 1884.

Cherry Blossoms

In 1912, the people of Tokyo gave Washington, D.C., a gift of 3,000 cherry trees as a symbol of friendship between the two nations. In 1965, First Lady Lady Bird Johnson accepted a gift of 3,800 more trees. Then, in 1981, the Japanese collected cuttings of these trees to plant where a flood had wiped out many cherry trees in Japan. More cherry trees were planted around the Tidal Basin in 1999. All of these trees share a common ancestor: a 1,500-year-old tree from Japan. Washington, D.C., celebrates the arrival of spring and the blooming of the cherry trees every year with a two-week festival.